*To E
Live in Joy*

30 Days to Joy

by Barbara Schreiner-Trudel

*In Joy,
Barbara*

Published by:

FriesenPress

Suite 300 – 852 Fort Street
Victoria, BC, Canada V8W 1H8

www.friesenpress.com

Distributed to the trade by The Ingram Book Company

I dedicate this book to my father,
Victor Schreiner.

Dad, I miss you!

Acknowledgements

I have been blessed in so many ways and I am deeply grateful for the journey that brought me to this point in my life. Living in a state of gratitude and acceptance has allowed me to heal, awaken and grow.

This book was made possible through the combined efforts of a few remarkable people. First, I thank my friend Oliver Guttorm Svendsen for the idea that became this book. I thank my dear Natasha Lefevre for her beautiful photography and her inspired layout and design. Thank you to my son Riley Anderson, my husband Pierre Trudel, and Renee Paser-Paull who edited this book, I am so grateful for their impeccable attention to detail. Thank you to my dear friend Joyce Laveist for believing in me, and the work that I do. Thank you all, I love you dearly.

Last, but certainly not least, Ernest Holmes, the author of The Science of Mind and the founder of the Centers for Spiritual Living. Studying his writings has inspired me to change my life for the better. Through my studies and then into my ministry, it is his infinite wisdom that has guided my life and taught me the power of my mind to create. I am forever grateful.

In Joy,
Barbara

Foreword

Barbara Schreiner-Trudel is a master with her gift of clarity. Whether it is through counseling one on one or speaking to a crowd, her ability to bring joy is evident. 30 Days To Joy is a prime example of how effortlessly she shares her wisdom with others. It is written in a gentle and inspiring way that is sure to bring joy to your life. I have had the privilege of being taught by Barbara and the honor of her becoming a dear friend. I found this book at a dark time in my life and working with it brought me into a lighter and more joyous place.

Nanci Miranda

Introduction

Welcome to a 30-day journey of transformation. Over the years, I have discovered the power of my thoughts and the impact they have on how I am feeling and what I am doing. I wrote this book as a tool that can be used to help you to begin to think in a new way. Each day there is a positive thought for you to contemplate. To begin, I invite you to set goals for the journey. Long term and short term goals will help you to get clear about the most important things in your life and will help you to focus on achieving them. Take the daily readings, read them aloud and use them as a guide for your day. When you read it in the morning, allow yourself to fully experience the words. It is written in the first person so as to make the experience more personal for you. After reading the page, set an intention for your day based on what you have read and revisit the page often during the day. Do your best to practice what is being offered. Bring it fully into your experience and watch the profound results that occur. At some point during the day take time to journal your experiences. The changes you experience in these 30 days may well be the biggest changes in your life so far.

You deserve the very best that life has to offer. Believe me, you are worth it. You will live in Joy once you accept that there is Just One You.

In Joy,
Barbara

My goals for the Journey

SHORT TERM

_____

_____

_____

_____

_____

_____

_____

_____

_____

_____

_____

_____

_____

_____

_____

_____

_____

_____

_____

_____

_____

_____

_____

_____

My goals for the journey

LONG TERM

_____

_____

_____

_____

_____

_____

_____

_____

_____

_____

_____

_____

_____

_____

_____

_____

_____

_____

_____

_____

_____

_____

30 Days to Joy

Daily Transformational Messages

Day 1

When I was born into this life, I was already a fully formed
person with a complete identity. My parents and caregiv-
ers were here to guide me and keep me safe.

The confusion came when my parents thought their job was to create a
doctor, lawyer, famous singer or whatever it was they thought I should
be. I realize this is not the task my parents were given, rather they
were meant to provide me with a safe and nurturing environment.

It is not necessary for me to do great things to be considered a
great person. Being myself and enjoying my life is more valuable
and healthy in the long run. Success is about the quality of life I
live, not the amount of fame or fortune I have. Today I choose
to be myself - in the end it will be the only thing that matters.

I experience each moment of my life. Some of these moments
I like and some I do not, and I know that all of them are
serving me in some way. I know this moment is the only one
I am guaranteed to have. I choose to live, love, and laugh.

My Experience

_____

_____

_____

_____

_____

_____

_____

_____

_____

_____

_____

_____

_____

_____

_____

_____

_____

_____

_____

_____

_____

_____

_____

_____

_____

_____

_____

_____

Day 2

There is One power in the Universe and whether I call it
God, Spirit, Higher Power or whatever name of my choosing, I know that it is everywhere present, all-knowing, and
all-powerful. With this in mind, I remember that I must be
One with It, if It is everywhere, It must be here where I am.

This is a powerful awareness. As I begin to see myself as infinite potential
I begin to live my life differently. When I live my life in harmony with
my natural gifts and talents, something wonderful happens...JOY.

My Experience

_____

_____

_____

_____

_____

_____

_____

_____

_____

_____

_____

_____

_____

_____

_____

_____

_____

_____

_____

_____

_____

_____

_____

_____

_____

_____

_____

Day 3

Acceptance of what is allows me to begin to live in greater happiness. As I take responsibility for what is happening in my life, I can creatively move forward. The reason for this is quite simple: if I created one thing, maybe a thing I don't like, I must also have the ability to create something different.

Life is a journey and resistance of what I am experiencing creates pain, whereas, acceptance of what is happening in my life creates joy. Sounds pretty simple, accept what is and live a happy life. I like it. I choose to live this today.

My Experience

_____

_____

_____

_____

_____

_____

_____

_____

_____

_____

_____

_____

_____

_____

_____

_____

_____

_____

_____

_____

_____

_____

_____

_____

_____

_____

_____

_____

Day 4

I live in an abundant Universe. If I look around me, I see abundance everywhere: the flakes of snow on the ground in winter, the grains of sand on the beach, golden leaves falling during autumn. Bounty. I can see it all around me, and yet when I look at the world, I see many people who are experiencing much less than what they need. Why is this? What is causing an experience of lack in a Universe filled with opulence? As I ponder this question, I come to realize it is fear that keeps me in this experience. Fear prevents me from sharing fully, fear prevents me from loving completely, and fear causes me to hoard what I have in case nothing more will come. So, how do I shift the fear? It starts with believing in something more than my current experience. It comes with a belief in Spirit or a higher power. When I believe in something more than what I see around me, I develop faith. Faith helps me to see the possibility of something more or at least something different. This moves me from fear towards love. I begin to realize that love and fear cannot share the same space at the same time. When love is present it eradicates fear. I believe that fear is an illusion and love is the reality.

F-false
E-evidence
A-appearing
R-real (Neale Donald Walsch)
or,
F-feeling
E-excited
A-and
R-ready

It is simply a question of perspective.

My Experience

_____

_____

_____

_____

_____

_____

_____

_____

_____

_____

_____

_____

_____

_____

_____

_____

_____

_____

_____

_____

_____

_____

_____

_____

_____

_____

Day 5

When a busy week has come to a close I choose to feel satisfied and grateful. When I look at how I spent my time during the past week, I sometimes tend to focus on whether it was spent wisely or wastefully. What would life be like if I simply released the past week's experience with a grateful heart, knowing that all things change and all is Spirit, keeping in mind that Spirit, or God, is always good? My feeling about my experience is changed as a result of my new perspective.

My Experience

Day 6

On my spiritual path, I may want to change something in my life.
Maybe I want a more satisfying career, or loving relationships,
improved health, or any number of other things. Why do I want this?
I think it will make me happy, or sometimes I think I want freedom,
relief and peace of mind, but happiness is my ultimate desire. When
I experience freedom, peace and relief, I am happy. Happiness
always exists within me and I experience this feeling now. Since it
exists within me, I can choose to experience it often. My natural
state of being is joy, and as a result of that Truth, I can call it up at
a moment's notice. Even in the midst of deep grief and despair, the
simplest things can cause raucous laughter. Being happy is natural.
Today I spend more time thinking about the things in my life that
are working for me and I find that happiness is my experience.

My Experience

_____

_____

_____

_____

_____

_____

_____

_____

_____

_____

_____

_____

_____

_____

_____

_____

_____

_____

_____

_____

_____

_____

_____

_____

_____

_____

_____

_____

Day 7

Today I think about where I focus my attention. Then I ask myself, "Does this add to my life or subtract from it? Is it moving me to where I really want to be?" If I answer "No" I change my focus. I choose to focus my attention on all that I love about my life.

My Experience

_____
_____
_____
_____
_____
_____
_____
_____
_____
_____
_____
_____
_____
_____
_____
_____
_____
_____
_____
_____
_____
_____
_____
_____
_____
_____

Day 8

The spiritual journey may seem arduous. Maybe I believe I have to work hard to figure things out? Possibly. Maybe the beliefs I hold about life in general, factor into the way I do everything I do? Could be. Maybe I hold beliefs about how broken I am and I am working hard at getting fixed? Might be. But, what if it didn't have to be like that? What if I could change my thoughts about who I think I should be and the consequence would be a life of ease, joy and freedom? Sounds good.

I am on a journey of discovery, a journey of finding my authentic self, a journey of uncovering, and awakening to my true spiritual nature. And, yes, it is easy, fun and interesting. I choose today to fully experience my spiritual path with ease and joy. So, beginning today, I choose to play, to enjoy life, to explore the world, to meet people, to discover my true identity, and above all, to love what I find.

My Experience

_____

_____

_____

_____

_____

_____

_____

_____

_____

_____

_____

_____

_____

_____

_____

_____

_____

_____

_____

_____

_____

_____

_____

_____

_____

Day 9

The Laws of the Universe are exact. I seem to understand and accept the physical laws more readily than the spiritual ones. Both are powerful and both are impacting my overall well being and success. I understand that if I defy the law of gravity, it will cause me personal injury. The same is true for the spiritual laws; when I go against the Law, the result is some form of pain. The spiritual laws are directed by my inner experience. What I believe about myself and what I believe about life is what manifests around me. The Universe always responds to me, by responding through me. If I want to change my reality, I need to begin by doing some spiritual housekeeping. This will quickly move me into a greater experience of love, joy and prosperity.

My Experience

_____

_____

_____

_____

_____

_____

_____

_____

_____

_____

_____

_____

_____

_____

_____

_____

_____

_____

_____

_____

_____

_____

_____

_____

_____

_____

Day 10

Health is such an important part of my experience and sometimes I take it for granted. Then something happens and I wake up to the realization that this body is a temple, so to speak. It is my mode of transportation during this life experience and it reflects my current consciousness. The body communicates with me in many ways. Aches and pains can be signals of needs unmet; disease can be the result of holding thoughts of resentment or guilt. Excess weight, perhaps, can be a desire to protect myself. When I treat my body with love and compassion I begin to hear the messages it is sending. Then I get to choose, to change my behavior, or not.

I love the skin I'm in, it is what I have for my current journey.

My Experience

_____
_____
_____
_____
_____
_____
_____
_____
_____
_____
_____
_____
_____
_____
_____
_____
_____
_____
_____
_____
_____
_____
_____
_____
_____
_____

Day 11

Life is a journey, filled with surprises and opportunities. As I pay attention to each thing I experience, the feelings and the thoughts I have, I become more conscious of how my life is being created. By living in the now moment, I open up to a deeper connection with Spirit and an awakening of my full potential.

My Experience

_____

_____

_____

_____

_____

_____

_____

_____

_____

_____

_____

_____

_____

_____

_____

_____

_____

_____

_____

_____

_____

_____

_____

Day 12

Love is the answer to every question, challenge and concern. Love is acceptance, love is respect, love is compassion, love is nurturing, love is freedom, and love is faith. When I accept what is happening, when I live in the present, and when I open up to inspiration, my life changes. The change is more of a deeper understanding, or an awakening of my authentic self. Living in the full awareness of my authentic nature is the most powerful experience possible. This is real and lasting love.

My Experience

Day 13

Getting along with people requires a little effort sometimes. It is
important to remember that I am a unique expression of Spirit. It
is also important to realize that this is true of all people. Knowing
that helps, especially in those moments when I am in a conflict
with someone I love. Sharing love, respect, and kindness goes
a long way in diffusing even the most difficult situations.

My Experience

Day 14

Think about Love and what it really is. I know something of romantic love but Love is something bigger, something more. Acceptance feels like a good fit. Acceptance is allowing people to be who they are and where they are in their lives. Acceptance allows the people in my life to do what they do without me judging or criticizing them. I also accept myself, where I am. I now live my life from this new understanding. Love is what I seek and it is also what I am.

My Experience

_____

_____

_____

_____

_____

_____

_____

_____

_____

_____

_____

_____

_____

_____

_____

_____

_____

_____

_____

_____

_____

_____

_____

_____

_____

_____

_____

Day 15

Today I sit in the silence and I find my authentic self, my inner wisdom.

My Experience

_____

_____

_____

_____

_____

_____

_____

_____

_____

_____

_____

_____

_____

_____

_____

_____

_____

_____

_____

_____

_____

_____

_____

_____

_____

Day 16

Many times on this life journey I will experience fear: fear of other people, fear of differences, fear of change. It is natural for me to have these feelings. I am an awakened soul and I accept the fear and move through it. I choose to return to Love.

My Experience

_____

_____

_____

_____

_____

_____

_____

_____

_____

_____

_____

_____

_____

_____

_____

_____

_____

_____

_____

_____

_____

_____

_____

_____

_____

_____

_____

_____

Day 17

My thinking creates my reality. Negative thinking can quickly move me into anger. A shift in perspective can easily bring me back to peace. I am always choosing my responses to the events that are happening around me. Today I choose to look for the positive; I choose to do my best to understand the perspective of others and I begin to create from there. This always improves the interactions I have with others.

My Experience

_____
_____
_____
_____
_____
_____
_____
_____
_____
_____
_____
_____
_____
_____
_____
_____
_____
_____
_____
_____
_____
_____
_____
_____
_____
_____
_____
_____

Day 18

I'm fascinated by the journey I am on. As I figure out this whole production called living, I begin to see how I am making it more difficult than it needs to be. Life is simple, joyous and interesting and yet often I am fearful and struggling. Why? Maybe I am unaware that there is an alternative way of being? The way I think determines the way I experience my life. Today I make a conscious choice to be positive, loving and generous.

I choose to live in joy. I choose to live in the easy flow of the Universe. I choose to change my experience. First, I think about life differently. Thinking creates the story and evokes the emotion, which then creates my behavior! What a cycle!

Today I choose to live in ease and joy.

My Experience

_____

_____

_____

_____

_____

_____

_____

_____

_____

_____

_____

_____

_____

_____

_____

_____

_____

_____

_____

_____

_____

_____

_____

_____

_____

Day 19

A new day, I am so grateful! Today, my intention is to experience joy, fully and completely. When I set an intention at the beginning of the day, I give myself a great launch for the new day. My intention creates my experience. When I get up tomorrow, I will set an intention for the day. For example, I intend to have a peaceful day, or I intend to be powerful today in all my interactions, or I intend to see the beauty in everyone I meet today. Today and everyday, I set clear intentions. The result is fantastic, as my intention is always realized.

My Experience

_____

_____

_____

_____

_____

_____

_____

_____

_____

_____

_____

_____

_____

_____

_____

_____

_____

_____

_____

_____

_____

_____

_____

_____

_____

_____

_____

_____

Day 20

Relationships are powerful and it is essential that I acknowledge the gifts of even the most difficult relationships I experience. The people in my life reflect who I am. They are mirroring for me what I believe; about myself, my life, my sense of self worth and my personal value. When I accept that each person is mirroring some aspect of myself, or some belief I hold, and when I am willing to see the gift of this awareness and the potential it brings to my life then it is easy to be truly grateful for everyone, especially those that bring me the greatest challenges. When I look at it from this perspective, it is easier to become incredibly grateful for even the most difficult relationships. What a gift! I am grateful for everything and everyone in my life.

My Experience

_____

_____

_____

_____

_____

_____

_____

_____

_____

_____

_____

_____

_____

_____

_____

_____

_____

_____

_____

_____

_____

_____

_____

_____

_____

_____

Day 21

Many people are experiencing great difficulties these days: financial disasters, relationship issues, health problems, and career challenges. What would it take to make a real difference in peoples lives?

I imagine that the thoughts I have create the feelings I have, and that these feelings lead to the behavior I exhibit. Ernest Holmes said, "Change your thinking, and change your life." When I focus on my problems, they tend to persist and get bigger. When I am grateful for the good things in my life and begin to focus my attention on the good, that is what begins to expand. I think a loving thought today, for others, and myself, and I watch the changes begin. I am responsible for what I think and feel, and I have the power to think a new thought. I have powerful, creative thoughts now.

My Experience

_____
_____
_____
_____
_____
_____
_____
_____
_____
_____
_____
_____
_____
_____
_____
_____
_____
_____
_____
_____
_____
_____
_____
_____
_____
_____
_____

Day 22

Today is a new day. Where I am is where I am. Accepting
this moves me into freedom, peace and joy.

My Experience

_____
_____
_____
_____
_____
_____
_____
_____
_____
_____
_____
_____
_____
_____
_____
_____
_____
_____
_____
_____
_____
_____
_____
_____
_____

Day 23

Forgiveness is a powerful tool that promises freedom. Forgiveness frees me from my suffering and allows me to live fully in the present moment. Forgiveness is a gift I give to myself. Forgiveness is a powerful blessing that releases all my past hurts. Forgiveness is not forgetting, although in time that may happen. It isn't condoning bad behaviors. It isn't for the other person, it is for me. I forgive myself, I forgive others, and I receive the blessing of forgiveness when it is offered. This is love.

My Experience

_____
_____
_____
_____
_____
_____
_____
_____
_____
_____
_____
_____
_____
_____
_____
_____
_____
_____
_____
_____
_____
_____
_____
_____
_____
_____
_____

Day 24

Although I am sometimes challenged by members of my family, it is true that they know me best and often times are most accepting of my bad behaviors, or at least are more forgiving. I choose to be grateful for the people in my life and all that I have learned and all that I know as a result of my relationships. I am grateful for the life I have lived up until now, and the life to come will be better than I have even imagined.

My Experience

_____
_____
_____
_____
_____
_____
_____
_____
_____
_____
_____
_____
_____
_____
_____
_____
_____
_____
_____
_____
_____
_____
_____
_____
_____
_____
_____
_____

Day 25

Focusing on the things I am grateful for shifts my attention from the problems I may be experiencing, to the things that are good in my life. What I think about, comes about; thinking about my good expands and increases it.

My Experience

_____
_____
_____
_____
_____
_____
_____
_____
_____
_____
_____
_____
_____
_____
_____
_____
_____
_____
_____
_____
_____
_____
_____
_____
_____
_____
_____

Day 26

I have been conditioned to fear almost everything. This conditioning is reversible. Today I see the beauty in the people I meet and I enjoy the love that is always present. I follow my intuition and I know what is good for me.

My Experience

_____

_____

_____

_____

_____

_____

_____

_____

_____

_____

_____

_____

_____

_____

_____

_____

_____

_____

_____

_____

_____

_____

_____

_____

_____

_____

_____

Day 27

A change of thought changes my reality. If I focus on what's wrong, I create unhappiness; when I focus on what I love, or what is right, I am happy. What a simple perspective to life!

My Experience

Day 28

Life is full of surprises. Some of them I really like and others,
not so much. Through this life journey I begin to learn that often
the toughest experiences bring me the greatest rewards.

My Experience

Day 29

I only have this moment and what I do with it matters. I choose to fully engage with the people around me. Feeling relaxed and peaceful I accept my life as it is. From this place I ask "Now What?" with excitement, and I know something good is on its way.

My Experience

_____
_____
_____
_____
_____
_____
_____
_____
_____
_____
_____
_____
_____
_____
_____
_____
_____
_____
_____
_____
_____
_____
_____
_____
_____
_____
_____
_____

JOY!

Just One You!

I am unique and precious and there is only one of me.

I am truly grateful for this knowledge.

Today I choose to live in joy.

My Experience

_____

_____

_____

_____

_____

_____

_____

_____

_____

_____

_____

_____

_____

_____

_____

_____

_____

_____

_____

_____

_____

_____

My goals accomplished

_____

_____

_____

_____

_____

_____

_____

_____

_____

_____

_____

_____

_____

_____

_____

_____

_____

_____

_____

_____

_____

_____

_____

_____

_____

_____

My new goals

_____
_____
_____
_____
_____
_____
_____
_____
_____
_____
_____
_____
_____
_____
_____
_____
_____
_____
_____
_____
_____
_____
_____
_____
_____

Barbara Schreiner-Trudel

BIOGRAPHY

Since 1998, Barbara Schreiner-Trudel has been coaching, speaking, and teaching, and she has helped thousands of people to live in joy. She has inspired people to create new careers, experience greater fulfillment, freedom, and peace of mind. Barbara has the capacity to create a safe environment for participants, and people leave her presentations inspired to take action. Barbara shares the tools necessary to shift lives into a place of real and lasting joy.

Barbara has lived in poverty and wealth, experienced the trials of teen parenting and the joy of having her fourth child at age 48. She has been in two violent marriages and is currently happily married. Barbara has been a single mom and is now enjoying the shared responsibility of parenting. Barbara was a high school drop out and later went on to college; she has gone from being angry to being a loving, peaceful individual. The bonus for anyone listening to her is that she can relate to your story; she changed her life and she can help you to do the same for yourself.

Barbara has earned the prestigious President's Award for Southam Inc. for outstanding contribution to the company. She worked as a cashier in a drug store, in advertising with the Calgary Herald for ten years, and at age 30 she went to college to study Journalism. Barbara produced and hosted two cable television shows, in the 90's: "Women In Crisis" and "The Barbara Schreiner Show". After eight years in a successful real estate career she started her ministry in Vernon, BC. In 2000 she founded the Centre for Spiritual Living, Toronto, and served as Spiritual Director for 11 years. Barbara is a Professional Speaker, Joy Coach, Author, and the Founder and CEO of Joy Here and Now.

www.joyhereandnow.com
info@joyhereandnow.com

Photo by Pierre Gautreau Photography